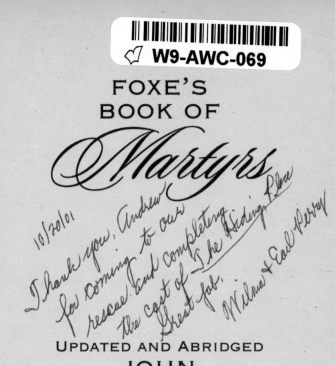

FOXE'S BOOK OF *Martyrs*

10/30/01

Thank you, Andrew for coming to our rescue. End completing the cast of The Hiding Plea. Great job.

Wilma & Earl Perry

UPDATED AND ABRIDGED
JOHN FOXE

BARBOUR
PUBLISHING, INC.
Uhrichsville, Ohio

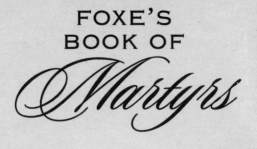

FOXE'S
BOOK OF
Martyrs

© 2001 by Barbour Publishing, Inc.

ISBN 1-58660-033-8

Published by Barbour Publishing, Inc., P.O. Box 719, Uhrichsville, OH 44683 http://www.barbourbooks.com

ecpa Member of the
Evangelical Christian
Publishers Association

Printed in the United States of America.

Contents

INTRODUCTION

John Foxe was born in 1516 in Boston, Lincoln-
shire, England. At the age of sixteen, he went to
Oxford where he received his bachelor's degree in
1537, became a professor, and completed his master's in 1543. Foxe was ordained a deacon of the
Church of England and worked for the Reformation, writing several tracts and beginning work on
his account of Christian martyrs, but was forced to
leave the country in 1553 when the Catholic Queen
Mary took the throne.

The first part of his book was published in 1554
in Strasbourg, France. He then went to Frankfort to
support John Knox's Calvinistic Party and moved to
Basel, Switzerland, where he served as a printer's
proofreader. Manuscripts and eyewitness accounts of
the Protestants' persecution under Queen Mary were
forwarded to Foxe in Basel and he continued to work
on his book, publishing the completed manuscript in
1559, the year after Queen Elizabeth I took the throne.
Returning to England, he filled in more details, translated the book into English, and printed it in March
of 1563 under the title, *Acts and Monuments of These
Latter and Perilous Days*. Becoming popularly

known as the *Book of Martyrs*, the text was widely read by English Puritans, shaping popular opinion about Catholicism for at least a century.

Foxe died in April 1587 and was buried at St. Giles Church, Cripplegate, London. His wife survived him by eighteen years, and they had at least five children.

This edition is a retelling of Foxe's major stories in modern English and should be readily understandable both by children and adults.

They overcame him by the blood of the Lamb,
and by the word of their testimony;
and they loved not their lives unto death.

REVELATION 12:11

PERSECUTION OF
THE EARLY CHRISTIANS

In the Gospel of Matthew, we read that Simon Peter was the first person to openly acknowledge Jesus as the Son of God and that Jesus, seeing God's hand in this acknowledgment, called Peter a rock on which He would build His church—a Church that even the gates of hell would not be able to defeat.

This indicates three things. First, that Christ will have a Church in this world. Secondly, that the Church would be persecuted, not only by the world, but also by all the powers of hell. Thirdly, despite its persecutions, the Church would survive.

The whole history of the Church to this day verifies this prophecy of Christ. Princes, kings, and other rulers of this world have used all their strength and cunning against the Church, yet it continues to endure and hold its own. The storms that it has overcome are remarkable. I have written this history so the wonderful works of God within the Church will be visible to all who might profit from them.

Of all people who heard Jesus speak, the Pharisees and scribes should have been the first to accept Him, since they were so familiar with God's law. Yet they persecuted and rejected Him, choosing to remain subject to Caesar, and it was Caesar who eventually destroyed them.

God's punishment also fell heavily on the Romans. Hearing of Christ's works, death, and resurrection, Emperor Tiberius proposed to the Roman senate that He be adored as God, but the senators refused, preferring the emperor to the King of heaven.

Tiberius became a tyrant, killing his own mother, his nephews, the princes of the city, and his own counselors. Pilate, under whom Christ was crucified, was sent to Rome and banished to the town of Vienne, in Daulphiny, where he eventually committed suicide. Agrippa, the elder, was even imprisoned by Tiberius for some time.

After Tiberius's death came Caligula, who demanded to be worshiped as a god. He banished Herod Antipas, the murderer of John the Baptist and condemner of Christ, and was assassinated in the fourth year of his reign.

Following thirteen cruel years under Claudius, the people of Rome fell under the power of Nero, who reigned for fourteen years, killing most of the Roman senate and destroying the whole Roman order of knighthood. He was so cruel and inhumane that he put to death his own mother, his brother-in-law, his sister, his wife, and his instructors, Seneca and Lucan. Then he ordered Rome set on fire in twelve places while he sang the verses of Homer. To avoid the blame for this, he accused the Christians of setting the fires and caused them to be persecuted.

In the year A.D. 70, Titus and his father, Vespasian, destroyed Jerusalem and all of Galilee, killing over 1,100,000 Jews and selling the rest into slavery. So we see that those who refused Jesus were made to suffer for their actions.

THE APOSTLES

The first apostle to suffer after the martyrdom of Stephen was James, the brother of John. Clement tells us, "When this James was brought to the tribunal seat, he that brought him and was the cause of his trouble, seeing him to be condemned and that he should suffer death, was in such sort moved within heart and conscience that as he went to the execution, he confessed himself also, of his own accord, to be a Christian. And so they were led forth together, where in the way he desired of James to forgive him what he had done. After James had a little paused with himself upon the matter, turning to him he said, 'Peace be to thee, brother,' and kissed him. And both were beheaded together, A.D. 36."

Thomas preached to the Parthians, Medes, Persians, Carmanians, Hyrcanians, Bactrians, and Magians. He was killed in Calamina, India.

Simon, brother of Jude and James, the younger, who were all the sons of Mary Cleophas and Alpheus, was bishop of Jerusalem after James. He was crucified in Egypt during the reign of the Roman emperor Trajan.

Simon the apostle, called Cananeus and Zelotes, preached in Mauritania, Africa, and Britain. He was also crucified.

Mark, the first bishop of Alexandria, preached the gospel in Egypt. He was burned and buried in a place named Bucolus during Trajan's reign.

Bartholomew is said to have preached in India and translated the Gospel of Matthew into their tongue. He was beaten, crucified, and beheaded in Albinopolis, Armenia.

Andrew, Peter's brother, preached to the Scythians, Sogdians, and the Sacae in Sebastopolis, Ethiopia, in the year A.D. 80. He was crucified by Aegeas, the governor of the Edessenes, and was buried in Patrae, in Archaia. Bernard and St. Cyprian mention the confession and martyrdom of this blessed apostle. Partly from them and partly from other reliable writers, we gather the following material.

When Andrew, through his diligent preaching, had brought many to the faith of Christ, Aegeas, the governor, asked permission of the Roman senate to force all Christians to sacrifice to and honor the

Roman idols. Andrew thought he should resist Aegeas and went to him, telling him that a judge of men should first know and worship his Judge in heaven. While worshiping the true God, Andrew said, he should banish all false gods and blind idols from his mind.

Furious at Andrew, Aegeas demanded to know if he was the man who had recently overthrown the temple of the gods and persuaded men to become Christians—a "superstitious sect" that had recently been declared illegal by the Romans.

Andrew replied that the rulers of Rome didn't understand the truth. The Son of God, who came into the world for man's sake, taught that the Roman gods were devils, enemies of mankind, teaching men to offend God, and causing Him to turn away from them. By serving the devil, men fall into all kinds of wickedness, Andrew said, and after they die, nothing but their evil deeds are remembered.

The proconsul ordered Andrew not to preach these things anymore, or he would face a speedy crucifixion. Whereupon Andrew replied, "I would not have preached the honor and glory of the cross if I feared the death of the cross." He was condemned to be crucified for teaching a new sect and taking away the religion of the Roman gods.

Andrew, going toward the place of execution and seeing the cross waiting for him, never changed his expression. Neither did he fail in his speech. His body fainted not, nor did his reason fail him, as often happens to men about to die. He said, "Oh cross, most welcome and longed for! With a willing mind, joyfully and desirously, I come to you, being the scholar of Him which did hang on you, because I have always been your lover and yearn to embrace you."

Matthew wrote his Gospel to the Jews in the Hebrew tongue. After he had converted Ethiopia and all Egypt, Hircanus the king sent someone to kill him with a spear.

After years of preaching to the barbarous nations, Philip was stoned and crucified in Hierapolis, Phyrgia, and buried there with his daughter.

Of James, the brother of the Lord, we read the following. James, being considered a just and perfect man, governed the church with the apostles. He drank no wine or any strong drink, ate no meat, and never shaved his head. He was the only man allowed to enter into the holy place, for he never wore wool, just linen. He would enter into the temple alone, fall on his knees, and ask remission for the people, doing this so often that his knees lost their sense of feeling and became hardened, like the knees of a camel. Because of his holy life, James was called "The Just" and "the safeguard of the people."

When many of their chief men had been converted, the Jews, scribes, and Pharisees began to fear that soon all the people would decide to follow Jesus. They met with James, saying, "We beg you to restrain the people, for they believe Jesus as though

He were Christ. Persuade those who come to the Passover to think correctly about Christ, because they will all listen to you. Stand on the top of the temple so you can be heard by everyone."

During Passover, the scribes and Pharisees put James on top of the temple, calling out to him, "You just man, whom we all ought to obey, this people is going astray after Jesus, who was crucified."

And James answered, "Why do you ask me of Jesus the Son of man? He sits on the right hand of the Most High, and shall come in the clouds of heaven."

Hearing this, many in the crowd were persuaded and glorified God, crying, "Hosannah to the Son of David!"

Then the scribes and Pharisees realized they had done the wrong thing by allowing James to testify of Christ. They cried out, "Oh, this just man is seduced, too!" then went up and threw James off the temple.

But James wasn't killed by the fall. He turned, fell on his knees, and called, "O Lord God, Father, I beg You to forgive them, for they know not what they do!"

They decided to stone James, but a priest said to them, "Wait! What are you doing? The just man is praying for you!" But one of the men there—a fuller—took the instrument he used to beat cloth, and hit James on the head, killing him, and they buried him where he fell. James was a true witness for Christ to the Jews and the Gentiles.

The first of the ten persecutions was stirred up by Nero about A.D. 64. His rage against the Christians was so fierce that Eusebius records, "A man might then see cities full of men's bodies, the old lying together with the young, and the dead bodies of women cast out naked, without reverence of that sex, in the open streets." Many Christians in those days thought that Nero was the antichrist because of his cruelty and abominations.

The apostle Peter was condemned to death during this persecution, although some say he escaped. It is known that many Christians encouraged him to leave the city, and the story goes that as he came to the city's gate, Peter saw Jesus coming to meet him. "Lord, where are You going?" Peter asked.

"I am come again to be crucified," was the answer.

Seeing that his suffering was understood, Peter returned to the city, where Jerome tells us he was crucified head down at his own request, saying that he was not worthy to be crucified the same way his Lord was.

Paul also suffered under this persecution when Nero sent two of his esquires, Ferega and Parthemias, to bring him to his execution. They found Paul instructing the people and asked him to pray for them, so they might believe. Receiving Paul's assurance that they would soon be baptized, the two men led him out of the city to the place of execution, where Paul was beheaded. This persecution ended under Vespasian's reign, giving the Christians a little peace.

THE SECOND PERSECUTION

The second persecution began during the reign of Domitian, the brother of Titus. Domitian exiled John to the island of Patmos, but on Domitian's death John was allowed to return to Ephesus in the year A.D. 97. He remained there until the reign of Trajan, governing the churches in Asia and writing his Gospel until he died at about the age of one hundred.

The church continued to grow, deeply rooted in the doctrine of the apostles and watered with the blood of the saints.

THE THIRD PERSECUTION

During the third persecution, Pliny, the second, wrote to the emperor Trajan, complaining that thousands of Christians were being killed daily, although none of them had done anything worthy of persecution.

During this persecution Ignatius was condemned to death because he professed Christ. Condemned to be thrown to the lions, Ignatius replied, "I am the wheat of Christ: I am going to be ground with the teeth of wild beasts, that I may be found pure bread."

THE FOURTH PERSECUTION

After a respite, the Christians again came under persecution, this time from Marcus Aurelius, in A.D. 161.

One of those who suffered this time was Polycarp, the venerable bishop of Smyrna. Hearing his captors had arrived one evening, Polycarp left his bed to welcome them, ordered a meal prepared for them, and then asked for an hour alone to pray. As soon as he had finished his prayers, they put him on an ass and brought him to the city.

As he entered the stadium with his guards, a voice from heaven was heard to say, "Be strong, Polycarp, and play the man." No one nearby saw anyone speaking, but many people heard the voice.

Brought before the tribunal and the crowd, Polycarp refused to deny Christ, although the proconsul begged him: "Consider yourself and have pity on your great age. Reproach Christ and I will release you."

Polycarp replied, "Eighty-six years I have served Him, and He never once wronged me. How can I blaspheme my King, who saved me?"

Threatened with wild beasts and fire, Polycarp stood his ground. "What are you waiting for? Do whatever you please." The crowd demanded Polycarp's death, gathering wood for the fire, and preparing to tie him to the stake.

"Leave me," he said. "He who will give me strength to sustain the fire will help me not to flinch from the pile." So they bound him but didn't nail him to the stake. As soon as Polycarp finished his prayer, the fire was lit, but it leaped up around him, leaving him unburned, until the people convinced a soldier to plunge a sword into him. When he did, so much blood gushed out that the fire was immediately extinguished. The soldiers then placed his body into a fire and burned it to ashes, which some Christians later gathered up and buried properly.

THE FIFTH PERSECUTION
A.D. 200

During the reign of Severus, the Christians had several years of rest, and could worship God without fear of punishment. But after a time, the hatred of the ignorant mob again prevailed, and the old laws were remembered and put in force against them. Fire, sword, wild beasts, and imprisonment were resorted to again, and even the dead bodies of Christians were stolen from their graves and mutilated. Yet the faithful continued to multiply. Tertullian, who lived at this time, said that if the

Christians had all gone away from the Roman territories, the empire would have been greatly weakened.

By now, the persecutions had extended to northern Africa, which was a Roman province, and many were murdered in that area.

THE SIXTH PERSECUTION
A.D. 235

This persecution was begun by the emperor Maximinus, who ordered all Christians hunted down and killed. Pammachius, a Roman senator, and forty-two other Christians were all beheaded in one day and their heads set out on the city gates. Calepodius, a Christian minister, after being dragged through the streets, was thrown into the Tiber River with a millstone fastened around his neck. Quiritus, a Roman nobleman, and his family and servants were barbarously tortured and put to death. Martina, a noble young lady, was beheaded, and Hippolitus, a Christian prelate, was tied to a wild horse and dragged through fields until he died.

Maximinus was succeeded by Gordian, during whose reign and that of his successor, Philip, the Church was free from persecution for more than six years. But in 249, a violent persecution broke out in Alexandria without the emperor's knowledge.

THE SEVENTH PERSECUTION
A.D. 249

By now, the heathen temples of Rome were almost forsaken, and the Christian churches were crowded with converts. The emperor Decius decided it was time to crush the Christians once and for all.

Decius, having built a pagan temple at Ephesus, commanded everyone in the city to sacrifice to its idols. This order was refused by seven of his own soldiers: Maximianus, Martianus, Joannes, Malchus, Dionysius, Constantinus, and Seraion. The emperor, willing to try a little persuasion, gave them time to consider until he returned from a journey, but in his absence they escaped and hid in a cave. Decius was told of this on his return, and the mouth of the cave was closed up, so all seven soldiers starved to death.

Origen, the celebrated author and teacher of Alexandria, was arrested at the age of sixty-four and thrown into prison in chains, his feet placed in the stocks which held his legs stretched widely apart. Even though Origen was rich and famous, he received no mercy. He was threatened by fire and tormented by every means available, but his fortitude carried him through it all, even when the judge ordered the torturers to prolong his suffering. During the torture, Decius died and his successor began a war with the Goths, which turned the empire's attention away from the Christians. Origen was freed; he lived in Tyre until he died at the age of sixty-nine.

THE EIGHTH PERSECUTION
A.D. 257

When Valerian was first made emperor, he was moderate and kind to the Christians, but then he fell under the influence of an Egyptian magician named Macrianus and ordered the persecutions to continue, which they did for the next three years and six months.

In Rome, Lawrence was brought before the authorities, who knew he was not only a minister of the sacraments but also a distributor of the Church's riches. When they demanded he hand over all the Church possessed, Lawrence asked for three days to collect it. On the third day, when the persecutor demanded the wealth of the Church, Lawrence stretched his arms out over a group of poor Christians he'd gathered together. "These are the precious treasures of the Church," he told his judge. "What more precious jewels can Christ have than those in whom He promised to dwell?"

Furious at being tricked, and out of his mind with anger, Lawrence's persecutor ordered him whipped, beaten, tied to burning-hot plates of iron, then laid on a bed of iron over a fire and roasted alive.

The first English martyr was a man named Alban, who was converted by a poor clerk who took shelter in his house. When the authorities eventually came for the clerk, Alban dressed in his clothes and went in his place. The judge recognized Alban and demanded he sacrifice to his heathen gods or die. When Alban refused, he was tortured and beheaded.

THE NINTH PERSECUTION
A.D. 270

This persecution began under the emperor Aurelian. Among those who suffered at this time was Felix, bishop of Rome, who was beheaded. Agapetus, a young Roman who sold his estate and gave the money to the poor, was seized as a Christian, tortured, and then brought to Praeneste, a city near Rome, where he was beheaded. These are the only martyrs whose names were recorded during this reign.

THE TENTH PERSECUTION
A.D. 303

In the beginning of the tenth persecution, which was in the nineteenth year of his reign, the emperor Diocletian appointed Maximian to share his throne with him, and the two of them chose Galerius and Constantius to serve under them. Under these rulers the Christians were again persecuted furiously, a state that would continue until A.D. 313, even though Diocletian and Maximian gave up their offices in the year A.D. 305.

Constantius and Galerius divided the empire between them, Galerius taking the eastern countries and Constantius ruling France, Spain, and Britain. Meanwhile, the Roman soldiers set up Maxentius as their Caesar in Rome. While Galerius and Maxentius continued the persecution for seven or eight years, Constantius became a supporter of the Christians in his empire, being an enlightened, intelligent ruler who was always concerned for the welfare of his subjects, never waging unjust wars or aiding those who did. Churches were terribly persecuted in other parts of the empire, but Constantius gave Christians the freedom to live and worship as they chose, even appointing them as his closest protectors and advisors.

Constantius died in A.D. 306 and was buried at York, England. His son Constantine, an English-born Christian, succeeded him—a ruler every bit as compassionate and dedicated as his father.

In Rome, Maxentius was ruling as a tyrant, killing his own noblemen, confiscating their goods for himself, and practicing magic—the only thing he seemed to do well. In the beginning of his reign, he pretended to be a friend of the Christians, but only to win popular support, while he secretly continued the persecution.

The citizens and senators of Rome soon grew weary of Maxentius's tyranny and wickedness and petitioned Constantine to come and free them. At first Constantine tried to convince Maxentius to mend his ways, but when that had no effect, he gathered an army in Britain and France and began marching toward Italy in A.D. 313.

Knowing he didn't have the support of his people, Maxentius had to rely on his magic arts and occasional ambushes of Constantine's advancing army, neither of which slowed Constantine's advance toward Rome.

But as he neared Rome, Constantine began to feel nervous about the coming battle. He'd seen Maxentius defeat others by the use of his magic, and he wished he had a force to use against it. One day at sunset, Constantine looked up to the south to see the bright form of the cross and the words, "In this overcome." He and the men with him were astonished at the sign, although no one was too sure what it actually meant. But one night as Constantine slept, Christ appeared to him with the same cross, telling him to make a cross to carry before him into battle.

This sign and its message wasn't given to induce superstitious worship of the cross, as though the cross had any power in itself, but as an admonition to seek Jesus and set forth the glory of His name.

The next day, Constantine had a cross made of gold and precious stones, which he carried before the army in place of his flag. With added confidence that God had blessed his cause, he hurried toward

Rome and the showdown with Maxentius.

Maxentius was now forced out of the city to meet Constantine on the far side of the Tiber River. After he crossed the bridge named Pons Milvias, Maxentius destroyed it, replacing it with an unstable bridge made of boats and planks, thinking to trap Constantine. The two armies clashed. Constantine drove Maxentius backward farther and farther, until, in his haste to safety, he tried to retreat over the new bridge and fell into his own trap. His horse tumbled off the unstable planking, taking Maxentius in his armor to the bottom of the Tiber, where he drowned.

Maxentius was the last Roman persecutor of the Christians, whom Constantine set free after three hundred years of oppression and death. Constantine so firmly established the rights of Christians to worship God that it would be a thousand years before they would again suffer for their faith.

For three hundred years, the strongest and richest rulers in the world had tried to snuff out Christianity, using force, politics, torture, and death—everything at their disposal. Now all those emperors were gone, while Christ and His Church still stood.

Persecutions under Julian
a.d. 361

Julian became emperor at the death of his brother Constantius, the son of Constantine the Great. Although Julian had been educated by his father in the Christian faith, he was at heart a pagan, and no sooner was he seated on the throne than he made a public avowal of his belief and trust in the ancient gods of the heathen, earning himself the title Julian the Apostate.

Julian restored idolatrous worship by opening the temples and ordering the magistrates and people to follow his example, but he did not make any laws against Christianity. He allowed every religious sect its freedom, although he exerted all the influence he could to restore the old faith. Although no violent deaths of Christians are recorded as resulting from any orders from Julian, several executions did take place around the empire on orders of heathen governors and officers.

Persecutions by the Goths

During the reign of Constantine the Great, the light of the gospel penetrated into the land of the barbarians. In northeastern Europe, which was then called Scythia, some of the Goths were converted, but most of them continued as pagans.

Fritegern, king of the Western Goths, was a friend of the Romans, but Athanaric, king of the Eastern Goths, was at war with them. The Christians living in Fritegern's area lived in peace, but Athanaric, being defeated by the Romans, took out his anger on the Christians in his land.

PERSECUTIONS BY THE VANDALS
A.D. 429

The Vandals crossed over from Spain to the north coast of Africa and defeated the Roman army there, conquering the whole country under their leader, Genseric. Since the Vandals were of the Arian sect, they abused the Christians wherever they found them, laying waste to all their cities and ruining every beautiful or valuable object they found. They even burned the fields of grain, so anyone escaping their swords would die from famine. They plundered the churches and murdered the bishops and ministers in many cruel ways. Often they poured rancid, filthy oil down the throats of those they captured, drowning them. Others they martyred by stretching their limbs with cords until the veins and sinews burst. Old men found no mercy from them, and even innocent babies felt the rage of their barbarity.

When a town held out against them, the Vandals brought great numbers of Christians to the town walls and killed them, leaving their bodies to rot under the walls until the town had to surrender to escape the plague.

TELEMACHUS

Rome was celebrating its temporary victory over Alaric the Goth in its usual manner, by watching its gladiators fight to the death in the arena, when suddenly there was an interruption. A rudely clad robed figure boldly leaped down into the arena. Telemachus was one of the hermits who devoted themselves to a holy life of prayer and self-denial and kept themselves apart from the wicked life of Rome. Although few of the Roman citizens followed their example, most of them had great respect for these hermits, and the few who recognized Telemachus knew he had come from the wilds of Asia on a pilgrimage to visit the churches and celebrate Christmas in Rome.

Without hesitating an instant, Telemachus advanced upon two gladiators who were engaged in their life-and-death struggle. Laying a hand on one of them, he sternly reproved him for shedding innocent blood, and then, turning toward the thousands of angry faces around him, called to them: "Do not repay God's mercy in turning away the swords of your enemies by murdering each other!"

Angry shouts drowned out his voice. "This is no place for preaching! On with the combat!" Pushing

Telemachus aside, the two gladiators prepared to continue their combat, but Telemachus stepped between them. Enraged at the interference of an outsider with their chosen vocation, the gladiators turned on Telemachus and stabbed him to death.

The crowd fell silent, shocked by the death of this holy man, but his death had not been in vain, for from that day on, no more gladiators ever went into combat in the Colosseum.

THE SPANISH INQUISITION

The Inquisition of the Church of Rome was, in its days, one of the most terrible engines of tyranny ever created by man. It may be said to date from about the year 1200, when Pope Innocent III sent his inquisitors among the Waldenses and other sects differing from the Church, and continued until 1808. In its course, it totally crushed any Protestants living in Spain: Its final count numbered 31,912 people burned alive and 291,450 imprisoned. In the eighteen years that the Dominican monk Thomas of Torquemada led the Inquisition, 10,220 people were burned and 97,322 punished with the loss of property or imprisonment. Although its main victims were citizens of Spain, there were others who became its victims, too.

JOHN WYCLIFFE

John Wycliffe, who lived during the reign of Edward III in 1371, was the public reader of divinity at the University of Oxford. In a time when few people were educated, he was well known for his scholarship in the fields of philosophy and religion.

At this time, Christianity was in a sad state. Although everyone knew the name of Christ, few if any understood His doctrine. Faith, consolation, the use of the law, the works of Christ, our human weakness, the Holy Ghost, the strength of sin, the works of grace, justification by faith, and Christian liberty were never mentioned in the Church.

Wycliffe, seeing Christ's gospel defiled by the errors and inventions of these bishops and monks, decided to do whatever he could to remedy the situation and teach people the truth.

This, of course, aroused the anger of the country's monks and friars, whose orders had grown wealthy through the sale of their ceremonies and from being paid for doing their duties. Soon, their priests and bishops took up the outcry, followed by the archbishop, Simon Sudbury, who took away Wycliffe's salary at Oxford and ordered him to stop preaching against the Church.

Nevertheless, Wycliffe continued speaking his mind to the people in his sermons. Some authorities at Oxford attempted to silence him; others gave him whatever support they could; the Church considered him a heretic and threatened his followers with excommunication. For some time Wycliffe was either banished or in hiding, but he returned to his parish of Lutterworth to die in 1384.

In 1415 the Synod of Constance declared John Wycliffe a notorious heretic who died in his heresy and ordered his bones removed from consecrated ground. In 1425 Wycliffe was disinterred, his bones burned and thrown into the river. But there is no denying truth, which will even spring up from dust and ashes. Although they burned his bones and drowned his ashes, the Word of God and the truth of John Wycliffe's doctrine would never be destroyed.

WILLIAM THORPE

William Thorpe was a valiant warrior under the banner of Christ. He was examined before the archbishop of Canterbury in 1407, accused of traveling through England for over twenty years, preaching his reform beliefs to the people.

The archbishop not only demanded that Thorpe deny his beliefs and return to the Catholic Church, but that he turn in anyone he found holding similar beliefs in the future. He was also forbidden to preach until the archbishop was sure he was truly converted.

"Sir," Thorpe replied, "if I agree to this, I would

have to be a spy for every bishop in England." Thorpe refused to pledge unconditional submission to the Church. "I will willingly obey God and His law," he said, "and every member of the holy Church that agrees with Christ."

What happened to Thorpe after he was committed to prison isn't known.

Poor Christians were being oppressed everywhere, but especially in England at this time, where the king supported the Catholic Church. The Church was so strong there that no one could stand against it; whatever it decreed was obeyed by all men.

JOHN HUSS

Richard II had married a native of Bohemia, and through her servants the works of Wycliffe were carried to that country, where they were effectively preached to the people by John Huss of Prague.

Pope John XXIII, seeking to suppress the Bohemians, appointed Cardinal de Columna to look into Huss's preaching and deal with any heresy he might find, so Columna set a date for Huss to appear before him in Rome.

Huss never appeared on the designated date, but King Wenceslaus of Bohemia sent ambassadors to assure Columna that any false doctrine being preached in his country would be taken care of by him, at his expense. At the same time, Huss sent his own ambassadors to assure the cardinal he was innocent of heresy. Columna refused all their pleas and excommunicated Huss for failing to appear in person.

The Bohemians couldn't have cared less about the proclamation of excommunication. The more they grew in knowledge of the Lord, through Huss, the less they cared for the pope and his rules. Although the Bohemian church officials succeeded in having Huss banned from Prague, he carried on his work, spreading Wycliffe's message among the people and causing a great uproar over the Church's riches and abuses.

In 1414 a general church conference was held in Constance to resolve the problem of the three popes and also deal with the Bohemians. Assured of safe conduct by both Emperor Sigismund and one of the popes, Huss traveled to the conference, arriving in Constance on November 3. Twenty-six days later, he appeared before the bishops to defend himself, but was not allowed to speak. In violation of the promises made to him, he was imprisoned for "safe keeping" and charged with eight articles of heresy.

On June 7, 1415, Huss was brought before a council and condemned as a heretic when he refused to recant his support of Wycliffe's theology. He was stripped of all his Church offices, made to wear a paper hat with the words *Arch-Heretic* on it, and led past a fire consuming his books.

On July 6, 1415, the hangman stripped Huss of his clothes, tied his hands behind him, then chained his neck to the stake. As the flames rose around him,

Huss was heard to say, over and over, "Jesus Christ the Son of the living God, have mercy upon me."

JEROME OF PRAGUE

Upset by the unjust treatment of John Huss, Jerome of Prague arrived in Constance on April 4, 1415, volunteering to appear before the council if promised safe conduct. This was denied him, so Jerome wrote out his thoughts on the council's treatment of Huss and had them hung on the gates and porches of Constance's churches and public buildings, then returned Bohemia, where he was captured and brought back to face the council.

Jerome denied that he had done anything against the Church, answering his accusers firmly and calmly, and was imprisoned for eleven days, hung by his heels with chains the whole time. Brought back before the council, he eventually gave in to their threats to save his life and agreed that John Huss had been fairly condemned as a heretic. Even then, he wasn't freed, but returned to prison under slightly better conditions. It soon became obvious that Jerome had given in to save his life, not because he had truly changed his mind about the council, and new articles of heresy were drawn up against him.

On May 25, 1416, after 340 days of imprisonment, Jerome was brought before the Council of

Constance and charged with 107 offenses, all of which he denied or disproved in short order, silencing his interrogators with his strength and knowledge of God's law. However, the outcome of the hearing was never really in doubt, no matter what Jerome said.

The Saturday before Ascension Day, Jerome was brought to hear judgment passed on him. He was given one more chance to take back his support of John Wycliffe and John Huss, but refused. The council condemned him as a heretic, excommunicated him, and turned him over to the secular authorities.

Jerome went to his death bravely, singing hymns, canticles, and the Doxology, then embracing a drawing of John Huss that he was bound to. Before the fire was lit, he said to the assembled crowd, "What I have just sung, I believe. This creed is my whole faith, but I'm dying today because I refuse to deny that John Huss was a true preacher of the gospel of Jesus Christ."

JEROME SAVONAROLA

Savonarola was an Italian monk, very well educated, who began to preach to the people against the evil living he witnessed within his own order, demanding reforms. As Savonarola's popularity grew, Pope Alexander VI ordered his vicar to proceed with the needed reforms in an attempt to silence the monk, but Savonarola wouldn't be silenced.

When the pope denounced Savonarola's testimony and ordered him to be silent, the monk finally realized the danger he was in and temporarily stopped preaching. But he took it up again in Florence in 1496 at the request of the people longing for God's Word. Cursed as a heretic, Savonarola told the people that such curses were against true doctrine and should be ignored.

Savonarola was taken from his cloister in 1498, along with two other friars who supported him, and burned as a heretic on May 24, 1499.

THE STATE OF RELIGION

By reading this history, a person should be able to see that the religion of Christ, meant to be spirit and truth, had been turned into nothing but outward observances, ceremonies, and idolatry. We had so many saints, so many gods, so many monasteries, so many pilgrimages. We had too many churches, too many relics (true and fake), too many untruthful miracles. Instead of worshiping the only living Lord, we worshiped dead bones; in place of immortal Christ, we worshiped mortal bread.

No care was taken about how the people were led, as long as the priests were fed. Instead of God's Word, man's word was obeyed; instead of Christ's testament, the pope's canon. The law of God was seldom read and never understood, so Christ's saving work and the effect of man's faith were not examined. Because of this ignorance, errors and sects crept into the Church, for there was no foundation for the truth that Christ willingly died to free us from our sins—not bargaining *with* us, but giving *to* us.

Although God allowed His Church to wander for a long time, at last it pleased Him to restore it to its original foundation. And here we must admire God's wisdom, for just as the Church fell into ruin because of the ignorance of its teachers, God gave man the art of printing, which restored knowledge to the Church.

Through the grace of God, men of wisdom were now able to communicate their thoughts accurately and widely, so others could distinguish light from darkness, truth from error, religion from superstition. Knowledge grew in science and in languages, opening a window of light for the world and clearing the way for the reformation of the Church. Still, many were left to suffer before that reform would be complete.

JOAN CLERK

In the days of King Henry VII (1506), in the diocese of Lincoln, a faithful woman named Joan Clerk was forced to set fire to her own father,

William Tylsworth. At the same time, her husband, John Clerk, did penance by carrying a fagot of wood, as did between twenty-three and sixty others. Those doing penance at Tylsworth's burning were then compelled to wear badges and travel to other towns to do further penance over the space of seven years. Several of them were branded on the cheek for their offenses. One of this group was a rich farmer named Robert Bartlet, whose farm and possessions were taken from him before he was locked in the monastery of Ashryge for seven years.

About the same time, Father Roberts was burned at Buckingham, while twenty others carried fagots for penance. Following that, over the course of two or three years, Thomas Bernard and James Mordon were killed and over thirty others were branded on the right cheek for speaking against idolatry and insisting on reading the Scriptures for themselves. Those to be branded were tied to a post by the neck while their hands were held immobile and a hot iron was put to their cheeks.

THOMAS CHASE

One of those persecuted for the gospel and Word of Christ was Thomas Chase of Amersham, a good man who often spoke against idolatry and superstition. Chase was brought before the blind bishop at Woburn and examined, and although we have no record of his examination, he must have professed Christ's true gospel against idolatry, for he was locked in the bishop's house in Woburn. There he remained in chains, manacles, and irons, all of which he took quietly and faithfully until they lost patience with him and secretly strangled him one day.

There would have been public uproar if the truth came out about how Thomas Chase had died, so the Church let out a rumor that the good man had hung himself. This would have been impossible, since Chase was chained in such a small area that he could neither sit nor stand, as a woman who saw him dead testified. To be sure no one would be able to examine the body, the authorities buried Chase secretly somewhere near the road between Woburn and Little Marlow.

JOHN BROWNE

John Browne ran into trouble with the Church by sitting too close to a priest on a public barge in 1517.

"Do you know who I am?" the priest demanded. "You're sitting on my clothing!"

"No sir," replied Browne, "I don't know who you are."

"I'm a priest."

"Oh. Are you a parson? a vicar? or a lady's chaplain?"

"No. I'm a soul priest," the man replied. "I sing for a soul."

"Do you? That's wonderful!" Browne exclaimed. "But where do you find this soul when you go to mass?"

"I don't know."

"Ah. And when the mass is done, where do you leave this soul?" continued Browne.

"I don't know."

"But if you don't know to find or leave this soul, how can you save it?"

"Get out of here!" the priest yelled. "You're a heretic, and I'll get even with you!"

As soon as he left the barge, this priest went directly to archbishop Warham. Three days later John Browne was taken from his home and imprisoned in Canterbury, where he remained from Low Sunday until Friday before Whit-Sunday, without his family's knowing where he was.

The night before he was to be burned as a heretic, Browne was locked in the stocks at Ashford, Kent, where he lived, and found by his wife, who stayed by his side all night listening to his story. Browne showed her his feet, which had been burned to the bones with hot coals by bishops Warham and Fisher, "to make me deny my Lord, which I will never do. Please, Elizabeth," Browne continued, "do as you have done in the past and bring the children up virtuously in the fear of God."

The next day Browne was burned at the stake,

saying, "Into thy hands I commend my spirit. You have redeemed me, O Lord of Truth."

1520–1521

As the light of the gospel began to appear and its number of supporters grew, the bishops became more vehement in their persecutions, causing much suffering in the land. Especially affected were the areas of Buckinghamshire, Amersham, Uxbridge, Henley, and Newbury in the diocese of London, as well as areas in Essex, Colchester, Suffolk, and Norfolk.

It must be understood that this move toward reformation began before the name of Luther was even known. England had always had godly people who were dedicated to the Word of God, sitting up all night reading and hearing and going to great expense to purchase the few books that were available in their tongue. Some would pay as much as a load of hay for a few translated chapters of St. James or St. Paul. Considering the scarcity of books and teachers, it's amazing how the Word of Truth spread as far as it did, neighbor teaching neighbor, sharing books and truth and so passing on the knowledge of God.

In the diocese of Lincoln, Bishop John Longland renewed the old persecution by bringing in one or two men who had previously recanted, and reexamining them. These implicated others, until a great number of people were brought before the bishop for the crime of assembling together to read the Scriptures. Those who were found to have relapsed were burned; the rest were so burdened with penance, that they either died from grief or survived in shame.

King Henry VIII made the bishop of Lincoln's task even easier by ordering all his secular legal authorities to give the bishop any aid and assistance he needed. Now both the law of the land and the law of the Church were against any who studied the Scriptures and upheld their truth.

MARTIN LUTHER

Martin Luther, born in Eisleben, Saxony, in 1483, was sent to the University of Erfurt. Here he learned the full meaning of Paul's statement, "We are justified with faith." Through his readings of the prophets and apostles and the exercise of faith and prayer, Luther came to believe the truth of Paul's statement and realized the error of what was being taught by the Church's schoolmen.

In 1508, at the age of twenty-six, Luther began teaching and preaching at the University of Wittemberg, impressing many educated men with his scholarship. Three years later he traveled to Rome about a disagreement among the monks, and was granted his doctorate, at the expense of the duke of Saxony, on his return. Luther soon began to compare the epistle to the Romans and the Psalms, showing people the difference between the law and the gospel. He also argued against the error that said men could earn remission of their sins through works, leading his listeners and readers to God's remission of sins through the love of Jesus, not through indulgences or pilgrimages.

All this time, Luther changed nothing in the ceremonies, carefully observing the rules of his order. The only way he differed from other priests was in stressing the role of faith in the remission of sins.

In 1516 Pope Leo X began selling pardons, by which he gained a large amount of money from people who were eager to save the souls of their loved ones. His collectors assured the people that for every ten shillings they gave, one specified soul would be delivered from the pains of purgatory. The pope's collector in Germany was a Dominican friar named Tetzel. On September 30, 1517, Luther put his objections to this practice on the temple adjoining the castle of Wittemberg. Tetzel immediately called him a heretic, burning his objections and his sermons on indulgences. Luther replied that he was not totally against indulgences, but preferred they be used in moderation.

Soon Maximilian (the German emperor), Charles (the king of Spain), and the pope contacted Duke Frederick of Saxony and asked him to silence Luther. The duke conferred with many educated men on the problem, including Erasmus, who supported Luther but urged a little more moderation in his writing and preaching. Duke Frederick communicated his concern to Luther but took no action to silence him. The argument continued, but in 1518 Luther wrote to the pope, totally submitting himself to his authority.

On August 7, 1518, Luther was ordered to appear before the pope in Rome. The University of Wittemberg and Duke Frederick immediately sent letters back to the pope, requesting that Luther be heard by Cardinal Cajetan in Augsburg. The pope told Catejan to call Luther before him in Augsburg, and bring him to Rome by force, if necessary.

Early in October, Luther traveled to Augsburg at the request of the cardinal, waiting there three days to receive a promise of safe conduct from the emperor. When Luther came before him, Cajetan rather gently demanded three things of him:

- That he repent, and revoke his errors.
- That he promise not to revert back to them.
- That he not do anything that would trouble the Church.

When Luther asked exactly where he had erred, the cardinal showed him Clement's papal bull on indulgences and maintained that faith isn't necessary to someone who receives the sacrament.

In his written reply to the cardinal, Luther stated

that the pope was to be obeyed as long as what he says agrees with the Scriptures, but that the pope may make mistakes, and any faithful Christian has the right to disagree with him if he is using better reason or better authority for his opinions. He also stated that no one is righteous and that a person receiving the sacrament must believe.

The cardinal told Luther to go away until he was ready to repent. Luther waited for three days in Augsburg, then sent a message to the cardinal that he would keep silent on the pardons if his enemies would do the same. He asked that every other point of conflict be referred to the pope for his decision. After three more days of waiting, Luther left Augsburg, but before he went, he sent a letter of explanation to the cardinal, along with an appeal to the pope, which he had published before leaving town.

In January 1519, Emperor Maximilian died. In October 1520, he was succeeded by Charles, king of Spain, who received the crown through the efforts of Duke Frederick. In November of that year, two cardinals arrived from Pope Leo to see Frederick and make two demands of him: that all Luther's books be burned and that Luther either be killed or sent to Rome. Frederick refused, asking for permission to carry on an investigation by educated men, which would determine if Luther was actually in error. If he were proved wrong and refused to recant, Frederick would no longer protect Luther; until then, he would.

In 1521, Luther attended the Diet of Worms at the request of the emperor and with his assurance of safe conduct. The fourth day after he arrived, he was ordered to appear before the emperor and other nobles of the German state, which he did. Told to keep silent until he was asked to speak, Luther was presented with two questions:

- Were the books gathered there his?
- Would he recant them or stand on what he had written?

Luther replied that the books were his work but asked for time to answer the second question. Brought back the next day, he said it was impossible to categorically defend what he had written, since he knew he was a fallible man, but he would be willing to be shown where he had made any errors. Asked for a simple yes or no answer to the two questions, Luther said he would stand on what he'd written until proven wrong by the Scriptures.

Unable to move him, the council sent Luther home under his safe-conduct pass. He was kept in hiding for a while, but eventually returned to Wittemberg where he died at the age of sixty-three after continuing to write and preach for an additional twenty-nine years.

ULRIC ZWINGLI

Ulric Zwingli moved to Zurich about 1519, living with the priests in their abbey, observing all their rights and ceremonies for two to three years, and instructing the people in Scripture.

The same year, Pope Leo renewed his pardons throughout the world, but Zwingli opposed them, finding proof in the Scriptures that they were wrong; he also opposed the other corruptions that were currently reigning in the Church. Finally Hugo, the bishop of Constance, wrote to the senate of Zurich and the college of Canons where Zwingli was living, complaining about him and warning everyone to beware of his teachings. Zwingli explained his faith before the senate of Zurich, which wrote back to the bishop in 1522, saying he should restrain the filthy and infamous lives of the priests and do nothing to hinder the liberty of the gospel.

Zwingli himself wrote to the whole Swiss nation. In his letter, he urged them not to oppose the advance of pure doctrine or bring trouble to any priests who had married. Since the Swiss custom was to allow priests their concubines, Zwingli urged them to allow them lawful marriages instead.

Zwingli continued teaching the Word of the Lord for several more years, the Dominican friars preaching against him, until Zwingli offered to debate with them. At this, the judges and senate of Zurich called all the priests in Zurich to a meeting on January 29, 1523, where everyone would be free to speak his mind. The bishop of Constance sent John Faber as his spokesman. At the close of the meeting, the senate of Zurich declared that the gospel of Christ should be taught out of the Bible and the traditions of man should be abandoned.

Soon the bishop of Constance wrote to defend the Catholic Church; about June 13, the senate rejected his doctrine and ordered all Catholic images in the city burned. The following April, the city of Zurich suppressed the Catholic mass, replacing it with the Lord's Supper, the reading of the prophets, prayer, and preaching.

Only Zurich took part in this reformation, not the other twelve cities of Switzerland, which remained with the Catholic Church. In December 1527, a meeting was called in the town of Berne where the two schools of religion were permitted to debate the issues freely. On the Protestant side were Zwingli, Oecolampadius, Bucer, Capito, and Blaurerus. The chief speaker for the Catholics was Conrad Tregerus, an Augustinian friar who tried to prove his points by sources other than the Bible, which was not allowed. Forced to stay within the Bible, Tregerus left the assembly. The arguments continued for nineteen days, with the end result that the city of Berne and those adjoining it abolished the mass, altars, and images of the Catholic Church.

In 1531, the cantons of Zurich and Berne, the

only two that had reformed their religion, were insulted by the other five cantons, which led to a war between them. When the five cantons refused to agree to a truce that would allow freedom of religion, Zurich and Berne cut off their roads, starving the cities, and forcing them to attack Zurich. Zwingli died in an attempt to reinforce a cut-off garrison of soldiers. His body was mutilated and burned by the Catholic troops. He died at the age of forty-four.

THE WALDENSES

About 1160, Peter Waldo, a citizen of Lyons, suddenly changed his lifestyle, giving away large amounts of money, studying God's Word, and teaching others how to live virtuous lives. In time, people flocked to him, eager to receive the Scriptures he translated into French and passed out to those who wanted to learn.

Soon the churchmen in the area, who would not explain the Scripture to the people, ordered Waldo to stop his work or face excommunication. Although Waldo ignored their orders, they persecuted his followers so badly that they were all forced to leave the city. The exiled Waldenses dispersed to many places, including Bohemia, Lombardy, and other French provinces. So perfect were they in their knowledge of Scripture that unlettered country men were able to recite the entire book of Job by heart. Others knew the whole New Testament. One of their fiercest persecutors admitted, "This sect of the Lyonists has a great show of holiness. They live justly before men, believe all good things come from God, and hold all the articles in the creed. Only they blaspheme the Roman Church and hate it."

Everywhere they lived for the next four hundred years, the Waldenses were subject to terrible persecution, especially in the year 1545. Finally, about 1559, the Waldenses living under the duke of Savoy in the Piedmont area were given freedom to practice their religion without persecution—after generations of patient suffering.

WILLIAM TYNDALE

William Tyndale was born near the border of Wales and brought up in the University of Oxford, where he studied languages, the liberal arts, and the Scriptures. After further study at Cambridge, he became the tutor of the children of Lord Welch, a nobleman of Gloucestershire.

Abbotts, deans, archdeacons, and other well-educated men often visited Lord Welch to discuss the works of Luther and Erasmus, as well as questions of Scripture. Whenever he disagreed with their positions—which was often—Tyndale never hesitated to defend his opinion with Scripture.

One evening, Lord and Lady Welch returned

from a dinner and told Tyndale about the discussion that had taken place there. Tyndale began to explain that what they'd heard was wrong, but was cut short by Lady Welch, "There was a doctor there who could afford to spend a hundred pounds. Another could easily spend two hundred, and a third, three hundred. Why should we believe you instead of them?"

At the time, Tyndale was translating Erasmus's *The Manual of a Christian Soldier.* When it was done, he gave a copy to Lord and Lady Welch. Once they read the book, they entertained the churchmen far less frequently.

Soon the area priests began to complain about Tyndale in the pubs and other places, saying his works were heresy and adding to what he had said to make their accusation to appear true. Tyndale was called before the bishop's chancellor, threatened, and charged with many things, but he was allowed to leave unharmed.

After this, Tyndale decided he'd better leave the area, so he traveled to London, hoping to secure a place with Cuthbert Tonstal, the bishop of London. When he was unable to do that, he left for Germany.

Tyndale, partly through the influence of John Frith, had decided that the people needed to be able to read Scripture for themselves, instead of trusting the Church to explain it to them honestly and fully. He believed that the corruption of the Church was tolerated only because people didn't know any better—

and the Church wasn't about to teach them any better, or its excesses and privileges would be in danger.

In 1526, Tyndale published his English translation of the New Testament and began on the Old Testament, adding prologues to each book. In addition, he published *The Wicked Mammon* and *The Practise of Prelates,* sending copies to England.

After traveling to Germany and Saxony, where he met with Luther and other learned men, he finally settled in Antwerp, The Netherlands.

When his books—especially the New Testament—began to be widely read in England, the bishops and prelates of the Church did everything in their power to condemn them and point out their "errors." In 1527 they convinced the king to ban all Tyndale's works in England.

Meanwhile, Cuthbert Tonstal, the bishop of London, worked with Sir Thomas More to find a way to keep the translations out of the public's hands. He became acquainted with Augustine Packington, an English merchant who secretly supported Tyndale, and Packington promised the bishop that he would deliver every copy of the translation's next edition, if the bishop supplied the funds for the purchase. When the bishop agreed, Packington explained the deal to Tyndale. Soon the bishop of London had his books, Packington his praise, and Tyndale all the money, part of which he promptly used to print a new edition that he shipped into the country. The rest of the money supported Tyndale for a while.

Tonstal publicly burned all the copies he had bought, an act that offended the people so much that the Church promised it would provide its own error-free translation. Nothing was done to fulfill this promise. In fact, in May 1530, the Church declared that such a translation was unnecessary, which immediately increased the sale of Tyndale's work.

Tyndale was eventually captured by the emperor in Antwerp, his books were all seized, and he was imprisoned for a year and a half before being condemned under the emperor's Decree of Augsburg. He was tied to the stake, strangled, and burned in Vilvorden in 1536, dying with these words: "Lord, open the king of England's eyes!"

ROBERT BARNES

On his graduation from the University of Louvain, Robert Barnes was made prior and master of the Augustines at Cambridge. At that time little literature was taught at Cambridge, but Barnes introduced its study and produced many educated young men who were familiar with the works of Terence, Plautas, Cicero, and others. Once literature was established, Barnes began teaching Paul's epistles, producing many good men for the Church.

Through his reading, discussions, and preaching, Barnes became famous for his knowledge of

Scripture, always preaching against bishops and hypocrites, yet he continued to support the Church's idolatry until he was converted to Christ by Bilney.

Barnes preached his first sermon as a Protestant at St. Edward's Church in Cambridge and was immediately accused of heresy. Brought before Cardinal Wolsey, his friends convinced Barnes to abjure, and he did public penance at St. Paul's before being imprisoned for a year and a half. On his release from prison, Barnes was sent as a freed prisoner to the Austin friars in London, but they soon brought more charges on him, and he was forced to flee to Luther in Antwerp.

While in Antwerp, Barnes became friends with Luther, Melancthon, the duke of Saxony, and the king of Denmark who sent him with the Lubecks as an ambassador to King Henry VIII. Sir Thomas More wanted to capture Barnes while he was in the country, but the king wouldn't allow him to, since Cromwell, his friend and advisor, had become the protector of the Protestants. Barnes was allowed to dispute with the bishops and leave the country at will. He returned to Luther at Wittemberg to publish his books, then went back to England at the beginning of Queen Anne Boleyn's reign, becoming a well-respected preacher.

Once Stephen Gardiner arrived from France, trouble fell on the Protestants again. From then on, religion suffered, as did Queen Anne and Cromwell, and Barnes was imprisoned in the Tower of London until he was burned on July 30, two days after Cromwell's death. Two other Protestants were burned with him—Gerrand and Jerome—plus three Catholics—Powe, Featherstone, and Abel. Seeing both Protestant and Catholic being punished for their faith at the same time confused the whole nation, although it was the political result of a division of the king's council, half of whom were Catholic, half Protestant.

THE LAW OF THE SIX ARTICLES

In 1539, at the instigation of King Henry VIII, Parliament passed the Six Articles upholding the Catholic doctrines of priestly celibacy and transubstantiation. The punishment for breaking this law was death, with no provision for recantation, although this was softened a bit by Parliament in 1544, which made provision for recantation and penance for the first two convictions and required death for the third offence.

At the same time, Parliament banned all of Tyndale's books and all songs, plays, and books in English that violated the Six Articles. The text of the Bible was forbidden to all women, craftsmen, apprentices, journeymen, servants, yeomen, farmers, and laborers. Noblemen and their wives were allowed to read the Bible if they did so quietly and didn't expound upon it.

Another provision of the Law of the Six Articles allowed a person accused of heresy to bring forward witnesses on his behalf, in equal or greater number of witnesses being called against him. This had never been allowed before in heresy trials.

KERBY AND CLARKE

Kerby and Clarke were captured in Ipswich in 1546 and brought before Lord Wentworth and other commissioners for their examination. At that time they were asked if they believed in transubstantiation. Admitting they did not, both stated their belief that Christ had instituted the Last Supper as a remembrance of His death for the remission of sins, but there was no actual flesh or blood involved in the sacrament.

Kerby was sentenced to burn in Ipswich the next day; Clarke the following Monday in Bury. When he heard his sentence, Kerby bowed devotedly, raised his hands and proclaimed, "Praised be Almighty God!"

The next day, Kerby was brought to the marketplace at ten in the morning, where the stake, wood, and straw were in place. He removed his clothing to his shirt, still in his nightcap, and was fastened to the stake with irons. Approximately two thousand people were present, including Lord Wentworth. After a sermon by Dr. Rugham, during which Kerby commented to the assembled crowd whenever he agreed or disagreed with Rugham, he was given time to say his prayers, which moved everyone, including Lord Wentworth, to tears. The fire was lit, and Kerby called to God, knocking on his breast and holding his hands up as long as he could. Everyone present praised God for Kerby's faithfulness to the end.

As Roger Clarke was being brought to the stake the next Monday in Bury, a procession of the host met them. Clarke refused to bow or remove his cap to the procession, vehemently rebuking such idolatry and angering the officers around him.

THE DEATH OF HENRY VIII

After a long illness, toward the end of January 1547, it became obvious to King Henry's doctors that he was dying. Although they felt he should know the state of his health, no one was willing to risk telling him. The task fell on one Master Denny, who boldly told Henry that he was dying and urged him to prepare for it by calling on God in Christ for grace and mercy.

The king listened to Denny and considered his sins, which he regretted, yet concluded that "the mercy of Christ is able to pardon me all my sins, even if they were worse than they are."

Glad to hear Henry thinking this way, Denny asked if he would like to speak to anyone. Henry replied that he would like to see Dr. Cranmer, but by the time Cranmer arrived, Henry was unable to speak and barely conscious. He was able to reach out and grasp Cranmer's hand, however. Cranmer urged the king to put his trust in Christ and call on His mercy, and Henry pressed Cranmer's hand as a sign that he was doing so, then died. Henry had ruled for thirty seven years and nine months, leaving behind three children—Edward, Mary, and Elizabeth.

PATRICK HAMILTON

The first Scottish martyr was Patrick Hamilton, abbot of Ferne, the son of Sir Patrick Hamilton of Kincavil, and Catherine Stewart, a daughter of the duke of Albany. Young Hamilton was educated at St. Andrews in the liberal philosophy of John Mair, then read Luther for himself. He was always noted for having a liberal mind and adopted Protestant theology wholeheartedly, but fled to Wittemberg when he was called to appear before an ecclesiastical council.

There, Hamilton became friendly with Luther and Melancthon, who recommended him to Lambert, the head of the University of Marburg. Lambert instructed Hamilton even more fully in Protestantism, which produced a great change in him. Where before he had been skeptical and timid, he now became courageous, almost rash, and decided to return to Scotland and preach the faith there.

He arrived back in Scotland in 1527 and publicly addressed the people for a time before being arrested and imprisoned. His youth—he was only twenty-eight—his talent, and his pleasant, gentle disposition, made many churchmen try to change Hamilton's mind, or at least convince him to stop preaching his beliefs and disturbing the Church.

Hamilton held so firm that he converted a Catholic priest named Aless who visited his cell. In time, Aless suffered persecution for his new faith, and was burned.

On the scaffold, Hamilton gave his servant all his clothing, comforting him by saying, "What I am about to suffer, dear friend, appears fearful and bitter to the flesh. But remember, it is the entrance to everlasting life, which none shall possess who deny their Lord." Even though his executioner's lack of skill prolonged Hamilton's suffering, he never ceased preaching to those standing near him. "How long, O God," he exclaimed, "shall darkness cover this kingdom? How long will You allow this tyranny of men?" He died with the words "Lord Jesus, receive my spirit" on his lips.

Henry Forrest

A few years after Patrick Hamilton's death, Henry Forrest preached that Hamilton was a martyr and what he'd proclaimed was true. He was put in prison by James Beaton, the archbishop of St. Andrews, who sent a friar named Walter Land to hear Forrest's confession. In his supposedly secret confession, Forrest affirmed his belief in Hamilton and all he had died for. The friar immediately went to the bishop and told him everything Forrest had confessed, which was used as evidence in his trial.

On the day of his execution, Forrest was stripped of his Church offices in front of the clergy, calling out, "Fie on falsehood! Fie on false friars! Revealers of confession! After this day let no man ever trust any friars, condemners of God's Word and deceivers of men!" He suffered death for his faithful testimony at the north church stile at St. Andrews.

James Hamilton, Catherine Hamilton, Straiton, Gourlay

In 1534, James Hamilton, Catherine Hamilton, David Straiton, and Norman Gourlay were called before King James V in Edinburgh. James Hamilton had been accused by the Church of holding the opinions of his brother Patrick. King James warned Hamilton not to appear at his trial, where he wouldn't be able to help him, but to leave the country and forfeit his lands and property to save his life.

Catherine Hamilton, James's sister and King James's aunt, was charged with not believing she could be saved by works. After a long discussion with a lawyer named John Spens, she concluded, "Work here, work there! What kind of working is all this? I know perfectly that no kind of work can save me except the works of Christ, my Lord and Savior!"

The king turned aside and laughed at her reply, then called her up to him and convinced her to recant for the sake of the family. She was set free.

Straiton was a gentleman from a good family, but he quarreled with the bishop of Moray over his tithes. One day when he was challenged by the Church collectors, Straiton ordered his servants to throw every tenth fish they caught back into the sea and told the collector to go look for his tax there. After this, he calmed down and became a sincere convert of the Reformation. Accused of heresy, Straiton refused to recant and was burned with Gourlay on August 27, 1534.

DEAN THOMAS FORREST

Every Sunday, Dean Thomas Forrest preached from the gospel, something that was normally only done by the friars. In retaliation, the friars accused him of showing the mysteries of Scripture to the common people, reading the Bible in the common tongue, and making the clergy detestable in the sight of the people.

Dean Thomas replied that preaching from the gospel once a week was barely enough, but the bishop maintained that they were not ordained to preach, admitting that even he didn't know the Old and New Testaments himself, being content to know his mass book and pontifical. At this time, nothing was done to Dean Thomas, even though he stood his ground and refused to stop preaching the Bible.

Shortly afterward, Dean Thomas was arrested, along with two friars named Keillor and Beveridge, a priest named Duncan Simpson, a gentleman named Robert Forrester, and three or four others from the town of Stirling. Accused of being chief heretics and teachers of heresy, none of them were given the opportunity to recant. The main charges against them were that they were present at the marriage of a priest and ate meat at the wedding, which was held during Lent. In February of 1538 or 1539, they were all burned in Edinburgh.

In 1543, George Wishart had been arrested and imprisoned in the castle of St. Andrew, locked in chains for his doctrine. On the day he was summoned to appear before the cardinal at St. Andrews, he was escorted to the church by one hundred armed men.

Despite his appeal, eighteen articles of heresy were read against Wishart, each of which he answered with Scripture that soundly supported his doctrine. When the bishops were through, they condemned Wishart to burn as a heretic, ignoring all his replies, and told the congregation to leave.

The fire was made ready and the gallows erected. The cardinal, afraid that Wishart would be freed by his friends, ordered all the castle's arms aimed at the gallows. Wishart's hands were tied behind him, and he was led to the fire with a rope around his neck and a chain of iron around his waist.

He told the assembled crowd not to let his death turn them from the Word of God. "I exhort you to love the Word of God and suffer patiently, with a comfortable heart, for the sake of the Word, which is your salvation and everlasting comfort." Then he asked the crowd to help his followers to remain firm in his teaching. "I don't fear this grim fire. If any persecution comes to you for the Word's sake, don't fear those who kill the body but cannot kill the soul. Tonight I will dine with the Lord."

After Wishart asked God to forgive those who

condemned him, the hangman kneeled before him. "Sir, please forgive me, I am not guilty of your death."

"Come here," Wishart replied. When the hangman went to him, Wishart kissed his cheek and said, "There's a token of my forgiveness. Do your job." As Wishart was hung and burned, the crowd mourned and complained that an innocent lamb had been slaughtered.

ADAM WALLACE

Adam Wallace was tried in the Blackfriars' church in Edinburgh before a large panel of priests, bishops, archbishops, professors, and civil authorities. His accuser was John Lauder, parson of Marbottle, clad in a surplice and red hood.

Wallace looked like a simple, poor man when he was brought in.

Lauder began: "Adam Wallace, you are accused of the following heresies. First, you have taught that the bread and wine on the altar are not the body and blood of Christ after consecration."

Wallace turned to the panel of judges. "I never taught or said anything but what I found in this book, which is the Word of God. If I was wrong, I will accept your punishment, but everything I said is from this book." Then he quoted Matthew 26:26–28 and Luke 22:19.

The charge was read again, and Wallace was

told to answer yes or no to it. "I only taught those who asked me to, and even then, not very often. What I said was that if the sacrament were truly administered and used as the Son of the living God instituted it, God was there."

Asked the same question once more, Wallace used Scripture to show why he did not believe the host could possibly be the physical body and blood of Christ.

The accuser went on to the second article. "You taught that the mass is idolatry, hated by God."

Wallace replied, "I've read the Word of God in three languages, yet I never once saw the word *mass* in it. If the mass is not founded on the Word, it's idolatry, which God hates. But if someone can show me the word in Scripture, I'll admit that I'm wrong and submit to correction and punishment."

The accuser continued. "You openly taught that God is just bread, sown of corn, grown in the earth, and baked by men. Nothing more."

"I worship the Father, the Son, and the Holy Ghost, three persons in one Godhead, who made and fashioned the heaven and earth and all in it. I don't know what God you worship, but if you show him to me, I'll be able to tell you what he is."

Wallace remained firm in his testimony, was sentenced, and returned to prison. On the day of his death, his guards warned him not to speak to the crowd, but many people said, "God have mercy on you" as he passed, to which he replied, "And on you, too." At the stake, he said to the crowd, "Don't be offended by my dying for the truth's sake. The disciple is not greater than his Master." The guards threatened him for speaking, so Wallace looked up to heaven. "They will not let me speak." The fire was lit, and Adam Wallace went faithfully to God.

WALTER MILNE

Among the martyrs of Scotland, Walter Milne was pivotal, for out of his ashes sprang thousands of others holding the same opinions, which forced the Church of Scotland to debate true religion with the French and the Catholic Church.

Milne was a parish priest of Lunan who embraced the doctrines of the Reformation and was condemned in the time of Beaton. He was able to escape safely from prison and hid in the country of Scotland until the leniency of the queen dowager allowed him to resume his preaching. Forced into hiding a second time, he was captured and tried for heresy at St. Andrews at the age of eighty-two.

The following dialogue took place between Milne and Andrew Oliphant, one of the bishop's priests, at his April 1551 trial.

"What do you think of priests marrying?" Oliphant asked Milne.

"I hold it a blessed bond; for Christ Himself maintained it, approved of it, and made it available for all men. But you don't think it's available for you. You abhor it while taking other men's wives and daughters, not respecting the bond God made. You vow chastity and break it. St. Paul would rather marry than burn, which I have done, for God never forbid marriage to any man."

"You say there are not seven sacraments."

"Give me the Lord's Supper and Baptism, and you can divide the rest among yourselves. If there are seven, why have you omitted one of them—marriage—and given yourself to immorality?"

"You are against the sacrament of the altar. You say the mass is idolatry."

"A lord or a king calls many to a dinner, then when the hall is ready he rings a bell to summon the crowd, turns his back on his guests, eats alone, and mocks them. This is what you do, too."

"You deny the office of bishop."

"Those you call bishops don't do a bishop's work as defined by Paul's letter to Timothy. They live for sensual pleasure and don't care for their flock. They don't honor the Word of God, but seek honor for themselves."

"You speak against pilgrimages."

"They are not commanded in Scripture. There is no greater immorality committed in any place than at your pilgrimages."

"You preach secretly in houses and openly in the fields."

"Yes. And on the sea, too, in a ship."

"Will you recant? If not, I will sentence you."

"I am accused of my life. I know I must die once and therefore, as Christ said to Judas, what thou doest, do quickly. I will not recant the truth. I am corn, not chaff; I will not be blown away with the wind or burst by the flail. I will survive both."

Andrew Oliphant ordered Milne given to a secular judge to be burned as a heretic, but the provost of the town, Patrick Learmont, refused to be Milne's secular judge, as did the bishop's chamberlain. The whole town was so offended at the sentence that they wouldn't even sell the bishop's servants a rope for tying Milne to the stake or a tar barrel. Finally Alexander Summerwail, more ignorant and cruel than the rest, acted as a secular judge and sent Milne to the stake.

When Milne was brought to be executed, Oliphant ordered him to climb up to the stake. "No," Milne replied. "You put me up there and take part in my death. I am forbidden by God's law from killing myself. But I go up gladly."

Oliphant put the old man up himself.

Then Milne addressed the crowd. "Dear friends, I suffer today for the defense of the faith of Jesus Christ, set forth in the Old and New Testaments. I praise God that He has called me to seal up His truth with my life, which, as I have received it from Him, I willingly offer to His glory. If you would escape eternal death, do not be seduced by the lies of priests, monks, friars, priors, abbots, bishops, and the rest of the sect of antichrist. Depend only on Jesus Christ and His mercy to save you."

There was great mourning and crying among the crowd as Milne died, and their hearts were so inflamed by his death that he was the last religious martyr to die in Scotland.

JOHN ROGERS

John Rogers was educated at the University of Cambridge, then served as chaplain to the English merchants living in Antwerp, The Netherlands. There he met William Tyndale and Miles Coverdale, both of whom had previously fled England. Converted to Protestantism, Rogers aided the two in translating the Bible into English, married, and moved to Wittemberg, where he was given a congregation of his own.

Rogers served his congregation for many years before returning to England during the reign of King Edward VI, who had banished Catholicism and made Protestantism the state religion. He served in St. Paul's until Queen Mary took the throne, banished the gospel, and brought Catholicism back to England.

Even then, Rogers continued to preach against the queen's proclamation until the council ordered him to remain under house arrest in his own home, which he did, even though he could easily have left the country. Protestantism was not going to flourish under Queen Mary; Rogers knew he could find work in Germany; and he did have a wife and ten children to think of, but he refused to abandon his cause to save his life. He remained a prisoner in his own house for a long time, but eventually Bonner, bishop of London, had Rogers imprisoned in Newgate with thieves and murderers and Winchester condemned him to death.

Early on the morning of Monday, February 4, 1555, the jailer's wife woke Rogers and told him to hurry and dress; this was the day he was to burn. His wife and eleven children met him on the way to Smithfield, but Rogers still refused to recant. Arriving at Smithfield, he was given one more chance by Sheriff Woodroofe.

"That which I have preached I will seal with my blood," Rogers replied.

"Then," said Woodroofe, "you are a heretic."

"That will be known on the day of judgment."

"Well, I'll never pray for you!"

"But I will pray for you."

A little before the burning, a pardon arrived, but Rogers refused to recant and accept it, becoming the first martyr to suffer death during the reign of Queen Mary.

JOHN HOOPER

During the reign of King Edward, John Hooper served as bishop of two dioceses, always acting as Paul instructed bishops to act in his epistle to Timothy. He never looked for personal gain, only for the care and salvation of his flocks, giving away any money that came his way. Twice, I (Foxe) saw Hooper's house filled with beggars and poor people who were eating at a table filled with meat, an event a servant told me took place every evening before Hooper sat down to eat his own dinner.

Hooper served as bishop for more than two years under Edward. When Edward died and Mary was crowned queen, Hooper was one of the first ordered to report to London and imprisoned. He remained there for eighteen months, gravely ill most of the time, forced to spend his own money to obtain food. On March 19, 1554, Hooper was called before the bishops of Winchester, London, Durham, Llandaff, and Chichester, and deprived of his bishoprics. On January 22, 1555, the bishop of Winchester called him in to demand he forsake his Protestant beliefs and accept the pope as the head of the Church of England. If he did so, he would be pardoned—as many other English churchmen had been. Hooper refused.

On January 28, 1555, Hooper appeared before Winchester and others and was given another chance to accept the Catholic Church. This was the same day that Rogers was appearing, and they met outside as they left the church with their guards.

"Brother Rogers!" Hooper exclaimed, "Should we take this matter in hand and begin to fry these fagots?"

"Yes sir," Rogers replied, "by God's grace."

"Be sure, God will give strength."

Hooper was returned to Newgate Prison for six days on January 29. On February 4 the bishop of London stripped him of all Church offices and Hooper was transported to Gloucester to be burned.

On February 5, Hooper was brought to the stake. He'd had been given packages of gunpowder by the guard, to hasten his death and lessen his suffering. These he put under his arms and between his legs. Three irons were brought to fasten him to the stake—one for his neck, one for his waist, one for his legs—but Hooper said they weren't necessary. Just the one around his waist was used.

After Hooper forgave the man who made the fire, it was lit, but the fire builder had used green wood, and even when it finally caught, the wind blew the flames away from Hooper. A second fire was lit, but it only burned low, not flaring up as it should have. When the fire was lit the third time, the gunpowder on Hooper went off, but even that didn't do much good because of the wind.

Even when Hooper's mouth was black and his tongue swollen, his lips continued to move until they shrank to the gums. He knocked on his breast with his hands until one of his arms fell off. Then he knocked with the other—fat, water, and blood dropping off the ends of his fingers—until his hand stuck to the iron around his waist.

Hooper was in the fire for over forty-five minutes, suffering patiently even when the lower part of his body burned off, and his intestines spilled out. Now he reigns as a blessed martyr in the joys of heaven that are prepared for the faithful in Christ.

RAWLINS WHITE

Rawlins White fished for many years in the town of Cardiff, a man who was well liked by his neighbors. During the reign of King Henry VIII, he was a good Catholic, but when Edward came into power, White became a great searcher of the truth. He was a totally uneducated man, unable to read, so he sent his young son to school, and when the boy had learned to read, his father had him read the Bible and other books to him every evening.

White enjoyed studying the Scripture so much that he soon gave up his fishing to travel from place to place and instruct others, taking his son everywhere with him. Although he never learned to read, White did have a remarkable memory and was able to cite from Scripture more accurately than many educated men of the day. He soon became a well-known, successful professor of the truth.

Five years after White began this work, Queen Mary took the throne. White gave up preaching openly, but continued to do so privately, bringing a great number of people to Christ. As the persecutions increased, his friends urged him to sell his goods, give the money to his wife and children, and go into hiding, but White refused to deny Christ.

The town's officers soon captured White, taking him to the bishop of Llandaff, who sent him to prison after having many arguments with him about theology. He was imprisoned in the castle of Cardiff for a whole year. Even though White knew he was doomed and his family would suffer terribly when he was gone, he continued to pray for and preach to the friends who regularly visited him this year.

At the end of this time, White was tried before the bishop of Llandaff. The bishop made a long speech explaining why White was being tried, to which he replied, "My lord, I thank God I am a Christian, and I hold no opinions against the Word of God. If I do, I want to be corrected by the Word of God, as a Christian should be."

After discussing the charges back and forth for some time, the bishop suggested they take time to pray that God would change White's mind. "Ah, now you're doing the right thing!" White exclaimed. "If your request is godly and lawful, and you pray as you should, God will hear you. So go ahead. You pray to your God, and I'll pray to mine. I know my prayer will be answered."

When they were done, the bishop said, "How do you stand? Will you revoke your opinions or not?"

"Surely, my lord," White replied, "Rawlins you left me, and Rawlins you find me. By God's grace, Rawlins I will continue to be. Certainly, if your prayers had been just and lawful, God would have heard them, but you honor a false god and pray incorrectly, so God didn't answer your prayers. I'm only one poor, simple man, but God has heard my prayer and will strengthen me in His cause."

As the furious bishop was about to condemn White, someone suggested they have a mass, to see if that worked a miracle in the man. Rawlins White left to pray in private while they went about their mass, returning when he heard the elevation bell ring—the principle point in the mass's idolatry.

"Good people," he cried to the congregation, "bear witness on the day of judgment that I did not bow to this idol" [the host].

White was condemned and returned to prison in the castle of Cardiff—a dark, horrible place. He was brought to his execution wearing his wedding shirt, an old russet coat, and an old pair of leather pants. On the way to the stake, he met his weeping wife and children, the sight of them making him cry, too, until he hit his chest with his hand and said, "Flesh, you're in my way! You want to live? Well, I tell you, do what you can, you won't win."

White went cheerfully to the stake, leaning against it for a while, then motioning to a friend in the crowd. "I feel my body fighting against my spirit and am afraid it will win. If you see me tempted, hold a finger up to me so I'll remember myself." As the smith chained him to the stake, White told him to tighten it well in case his body struggled with his soul.

They began to pile the straw and wood around White, who reached down and helped them pile it up the best he could, When a priest stood next to him to preach to the crowd, he listened respectfully until the man reached the sacrament of the altar, then called out, "Don't listen to this false prophet!"

The fire was lit. White held his hands in the flames until his sinews shrunk and the fat dropped away, only taking them out once to wipe his face with the fire. All the while he was suffering—which was longer than usual—he cried loudly, "O Lord, receive my soul. O Lord, receive my spirit!" until he could no longer open his mouth. At last the fire consumed his legs and his whole body fell over into the flames. Rawlins White died for testifying of God's truth and was rewarded the crown of everlasting life.

GEORGE MARSH

George Marsh lived quietly for many years with his wife and children on a farm in the countryside. When his wife died, he attended the University of Cambridge to become a minister, serving for a while as Lawrence Sanders's curate. Marsh preached for some time before being arrested and imprisoned for four months by the bishop of Chester, who did not allow him any visitors and had the names of any who asked for Marsh reported to him.

He was brought before Dr. Cotes several times but maintained the theology he had been taught during Edward's reign and would not be moved, although he did admit, "I want to live as much as you do. But I cannot deny my master, Christ, or He will deny me before His Father in heaven." Marsh was condemned as a heretic and turned over to the sheriffs.

Since he wasn't allowed any visitors in prison, Marsh's friends would stand by a hole in the outer prison wall and call out, asking how he was. He always replied that he was fine, anxious to die as a witness of God's truth and trusting Him to help him bear it bravely. On the day of his execution, Marsh was brought out in irons. Some people tried to hand him money, which criminals being executed would accept to bribe a priest to say masses for them, but Marsh told them to give their money to prisoners or the poor, not him.

Outside the city near Spittle-Boughton, by the stake, the deputy chamberlain of Chester showed Marsh the pardon he could receive from the queen if he recanted. Marsh said he would love to accept it, that he even loved the queen, but he could not recant.

The fire was poorly made, so Marsh suffered

terribly, bearing it with patience. He had been in the fire for a long time—his flesh broiled and puffed up so much that the chain around him couldn't been seen—when he suddenly spread his arms and called, "Father of heaven, have mercy on me" and died. Many people who witnessed Marsh's death said he was a martyr who died with patience and godliness, which caused the bishop to preach a sermon saying that Marsh was a heretic, burned like a heretic, and was now a firebrand in hell.

THOMAS HAWKES

On February 8, 1555, six men were brought before Bishop Bonner: Stephen Knight, William Pigot, Thomas Tomkins, John Lawrence, William Hunter, and Thomas Hawkes. All of them were condemned the following day.

A little before his death, some of Hawkes' friends asked him a favor. They were afraid for their own lives and wondered how long faith could stand in the midst of the fire. Hawkes agreed to lift his hand over his head if the pain was tolerable and his mind was still at peace. When he had been in the fire so long that he could no longer speak, his skin had shrunk, his fingers had been burned off, and everyone thought he was dead, Hawke's suddenly raised his burning hands over his head, and clapped them together three times. The people there—especially those who understood his gesture—broke into shouts of praise and applause as Thomas Hawkes sunk down into the fire and gave up his spirit.

JAMES ABBEYS

One of the many who labored to keep his conscience clear in those troublesome times was James Abbeys, a young man forced to wander from place to place to avoid being arrested for practicing his faith. But when the time came that the Lord had another type of service for him, Abbeys was captured and brought before Doctor Hopton, the bishop of Norwich.

The bishop examined Abbeys on his religion, using both threats and promises, until Abbeys finally yielded to the persuasion. When he was dismissed and about to leave the bishop, Abbeys was called back and given a sum of money, but once he left, his conscience bothered him terribly, since he knew he'd displeased the Lord by his actions.

Abbeys immediately returned to the bishop, threw the money at him, and said he was sorry he'd recanted and accepted the gift. The bishop and his chaplains went back to work, but this time Abbeys stood firm and was burned to ashes on August 2, 1555.

Bishop Latimer

Bishop Latimer was the son of Hugh Latimer of Thurcaston, Leicester, a farmer with a good reputation. At the age of four, he was sent to school and trained in literature; at fourteen he entered the University of Cambridge to study divinity, becoming a scrupulously observant Catholic priest. At first Latimer was a bitter enemy of the Protestants, opposing the works of Philip Melancthon and Master Stafford. But Thomas Bilney felt pity for Latimer and decided to try to win him to the true knowledge of Christ. Bilney asked Latimer to hear his confession of faith, and Latimer was so moved by what he heard, that he left his study of the Catholic doctors to learn true divinity. Where before he was an enemy of Christ, he now became a zealous seeker of Him, even asking Stafford's forgiveness before that man died.

In 1529 a great number of friars and doctors of divinity from all schools at Cambridge began to preach against Latimer and his new beliefs. Doctor West, bishop of Ely, forbade him to preach within the churches of that university, but Dr. Barnes, the prior of the Augustine friars, licensed Latimer to preach in his church. Like a true disciple, Latimer spent the next three years working to convert his brothers at the university and the parishioners of his church speaking Latin to the educated and English to the common people.

Latimer and Bilney stayed at Cambridge for some time, having many conversations together; the place they walked soon became known as Heretic's Hill. Both of them set a good Christian example by visiting prisoners, helping the needy, and feeding the hungry.

After preaching and teaching at Cambridge for three years, Latimer was called before the cardinal for heresy. At this time he bent to the will of the Church and was allowed to return to the university, where he met Dr. Buts, Henry VIII's doctor and supporter. Latimer joined Buts in Henry's court for some time, preaching in London, but became tired of court life and accepted a position in West Kingston that was offered him by the king. There he diligently instructed his parish and everyone in the nearby countryside.

It didn't take Latimer long to infuriate a good number of country priests and higher Church doctors with his beliefs on reform. Latimer was called before William Warham, archbishop of Canterbury, and John Stokesley, bishop of London, on January 29, 1531. He was kept in London for some time, being called for examination three times a week, until he wrote to the archbishop and said he was too ill to see him anymore. In the same letter, Latimer complained that he was being kept from his parish without just cause, for preaching the truth about certain abuses within the Church. Eventually Latimer seems to have accepted the charges against him (although there is no proof of this), and he was freed through the efforts of Buts, Cromwell, and the king.

In time, Henry VIII made Latimer the bishop of Worcester, where he served faithfully, although the dangerous times prevented him from doing everything he wanted to. He wasn't able to rid his diocese of its superstitions, but did what he could within the Catholic Church, helping his parishioners exclude as much superstition as possible from their lives and worship. Even then, he continued to be harassed by other members of the clergy.

When the Six Articles were passed, Latimer voluntarily resigned his post, as did Shaxton, the bishop of Salisbury. Latimer went to London, where he was harassed by the bishops and imprisoned in the Tower until King Edward took the throne. On his release, Latimer went back to work, preaching twice every Sunday and once every weekday, unlike many clergymen who ignored their duties during Edward's reign. He was now sixty-seven years old and suffering from an injury received by the fall of a tree.

Not long after King Edward's death, Latimer was arrested on Queen Mary's command and thrown back into the Tower of London, where he suffered greatly. He was transferred to Oxford with Cranmer, the archbishop of Canterbury, and Ridley, bishop of London, to answer charges made by Gardiner, the bishop of Winchester.

Because of his age, Latimer wrote less than

Ridley and Cranmer while in prison, devoting himself more to prayer. He prayed about three main concerns:

- Since God had appointed him a preacher, Latimer asked Him for the grace to stand to his doctrine until death.
- He asked God to restore His gospel to England once again.
- He prayed for the assession of Elizabeth, asking God to make her a comfort to the comfortless realm of England.

In time all three of Latimer's prayers would be answered, but not before he suffered at the stake and died a fiery death.

THE SPURGES, CAVILL, AMBROSE, DRAKE AND TIMS

These six men lived in the county of Essex. Being accused of heresy, they were all arrested and sent up to Bishop Gardiner of London, who sent the first four to Marshalsea Prison and the last two to the King's Bench.

After having been confined for a year, they were all brought into the court at St. Paul's Church to be examined by Bishop Bonner. Bonner began his examination with Tims, whom he called the ringleader, telling him he had taught the others heresies, and made them as guilty as himself. After talking this way for a while, the bishop asked Tims to submit himself to the Church.

In answer to this, Tims reminded the bishop that he himself had formerly given up the very Church he now professed such a love for, during the reign of Henry VIII. "My Lord, that which you have written against the supremacy of the pope can be proved true by Scripture. What you are doing now is contrary to the Word of God, as I can show." At this, Bonner called Tims an obstinate heretic, and condemned him.

Drake's trial came next. He frankly declared that he denied the authority of the pope and no persuasion would change his mind. No time was wasted in condemning Drake and turning him over to the secular authorities for punishment. The four remaining prisoners, Thomas and Richard Spurg, George Ambrose, and John Cavill, were then asked if they would forsake their heresies and return to the Church. They all refused to acknowledge any wrongdoing and declined to change their beliefs.

On April 14, 1556, the six men were taken to Smithfield, where they were chained to the same stake and burned in one fire. They patiently submitted themselves to the flames and quietly resigned their souls to that Redeemer for whose sake they had given their bodies to be burned.

HUGH LAVEROCK
AND JOHN APPRICE

Hugh Laverock was a painter by trade, living in the parish of Barking, Essex. At the time of his arrest he was sixty-eight years old and very infirm. Being accused of heresy by some of his neighbors, he and John Apprice, a poor blind man, were taken before Bonner to be examined.

Bonner asked the prisoners the usual questions, to which they answered without making the slightest effort to conceal their opinions. One week after they had been sentenced, they were taken to Stratford-le-Bow, the place appointed for their execution. As soon as they arrived at the stake, Laverock threw away his crutch, and spoke to Apprice. "Be of good comfort, brother, for the bishop of London is our good physician. He will cure us both shortly, you of your blindness and me of my lameness." Then they both knelt down and prayed earnestly that God would enable them to pass with Christian resolution through the fiery trial. These two poor old men—one a cripple and the other blind—were then chained to one stake, and the fagots lighted. They endured their sufferings with great fortitude and cheerfully yielded up their lives for their faith.

Catherine Hut, Joan Hornes, and Elizabeth Thackvill

These three women were arrested on suspicion of heresy and taken before Sir John Mordaunt and Mr. Tyrrel, justices of the peace for the county of Essex. After a hearing they were sent as prisoners to the bishop of London for refusing to attend the services of the Catholic Church.

The three prisoners were brought before the bishop and asked the normal questions to which they replied they believed in the reformed faith. Refusing to recant, they were sentenced to be burned and were delivered to the sheriff of London, who put them in Newgate prison until their execution. On the appointed day, they were carried to Smithfield, fastened to one stake, and burned together for their faith.

The Thirteen

Thirteen people who lived in the county of Essex were arrested in May 1556, and sent to London to be examined by Bishop Bonner: Ralph Jackson, Henry Adlington, Lyon Cawch, William Halliwell, George Searles, John Routh, John Derifall, Henry Wye, Edmund Hurst, Laurence Parnam, Thomas Bower, Elizabeth Pepper, and Agnes George.

On the Sunday after their condemnation, Dr.

Fecknam, dean of St. Paul's, said that the thirteen "held as many different beliefs as there were faces among them." This being reported to them, they drew up one confession of faith that they all signed. Early in the morning of June 28, 1556, all thirteen were taken from Newgate to Stratford-le-Bow, where the sheriff separated them into two groups and told each group that the other had recanted. When he found this strategy wouldn't work, he continued with the execution.

The eleven men were tied to three stakes, but the two women were in the middle, not tied to any stake. All burned together in one fire.

JOAN WASTE

This poor woman, having become a convert to the reformed faith, bought a New Testament and paid a small sum daily to an old man who came and read it to her, since she was blind. By this means and through her unusual memory, she became so familiar with the Bible that she could repeat entire chapters by heart. When she refused to attend services in the Catholic Church, Joan was brought before Dr. Ralph Bayn, bishop of Litchfield and Coventry, and Dr. Draycott, the chancellor, charged with heresy and committed to the prison of Derby.

She was examined several times by Peter Finch, the bishop's official, and afterwards brought to public examination before the bishop, his chancellor, and several of the queen's commissioners. The poor woman answered that she could not forsake the truth and begged them to cease troubling her. Finding that she would say nothing else, the sentence of death was finally pronounced and she was handed over to the sheriff. On August 1, 1556, she was led to the stake. As soon as she came to it, she kneeled down and repeated a prayer, desiring the spectators to pray for her. Having finished, she arose and was fastened to the stake, and when the fagots were lighted, the flames soon took away her speech and her life.

JOHN HULLIER

John Hullier came from a respectable family and was sent to Eton and King's College, Cambridge, where he devoted himself to the study of theology, intending to become a minister. After he graduated, he became the curate at Babram, a village about three miles from Cambridge. He hadn't been there long before he went to Lynn, where he had some dispute with the authorities. They reported Hullier's sayings to Dr. Thurlby, bishop of the diocese, who sent for him and, after a short examination, committed him to the castle of Cambridge.

A short time after this he was called to appear at St. Mary's Church before several doctors of law and divinity, by whom he was reproved. His examination being finished, he was ordered to recant what they called his erroneous opinions. This he refused to do. Without any loss of time, he was degraded, condemned, and delivered over to the sheriff, who immediately seized all his books, papers, and writings.

On the day appointed for Hullier's execution, he was led to the stake outside the town. He called on the spectators to pray for him and to bear witness that he died for the truth. One of the proctors of the university and some of the fellows of Trinity College were displeased at his addressing the people and reproved the mayor for allowing him to speak. Hullier took no notice of this, but being chained to the stake, he earnestly prayed to be strengthened to undergo the fiery trial. As soon as the fagots were lit, a number of his books were thrown into the midst of the flames, among them a communion book that Hullier caught joyfully and held in his hand and looked at as long as he could.

John Hullier's death was greatly lamented by many of the people, who prayed for him, and showed their sorrow by tears, he having been a kind and charitable man.

THOMAS HUDSON

Thomas Hudson was a glover by trade, living in the town of Ailesham, in Norfolk. Although he had little schooling, he was a great student of the Scriptures and preached on Sundays to any of his neighbors who were interested in hearing the Bible read and explained.

When Queen Mary began her reign, all unlicensed ministers who publicly preached to the people became marked men. Hudson would have been among the first to be arrested and thrown into prison, if he had not fled from his home. He traveled to Suffolk and by constantly changing his lodgings from one house to another escaped arrest.

But after a time Hudson's desire to see his wife and family became too strong to be resisted. In spite of the danger, he went home. Soon he heard that his enemies knew of his return, so he left his house and built a crude shelter beneath a pile of nearby firewood, only coming out in the darkness. This worked until the town's vicar threatened to burn Mrs. Hudson for hiding her husband. Hudson left his hiding place and openly walked into town, where he was arrested.

The bishop asked Hudson a great number of questions, all of which he answered honestly, and though he wasn't an educated man, Hudson's arguments were very strong. Finding he couldn't do anything with the man, the bishop finally condemned him and sent him to prison.

On May 19, 1558, Thomas Hudson was taken out of prison and led to a place called the Lollards' Pit, just outside the bishop's gate at Norwich, along with two other condemned men. Just before the chain around him was made fast, Hudson stooped, slipped out from under the chain, and stood a little to one side. This caused many to wonder if he was about to recant, or if he was coming forward for his parents' blessing. But no one knew the real reason: Hudson had suddenly been afflicted with doubts and felt his faith growing weak. Therefore, not willing to die while feeling this way, he fell upon his knees and prayed to God, who sent him comfort. Then he rose with great joy, as a reborn man, and cried, "Now, thank God, I am strong, and care not what man can do unto me." So going to the stake again, he put the chain around himself, and they were all burned together.

THE DEATH OF QUEEN MARY

After a long illness, Queen Mary died on November 17, 1558, at three or four in the morning, yielding her life to nature and her kingdom to her sister Elizabeth.

Hearing her sighs before she died, her council asked if she was sad about the death of her husband. "Indeed, that may be one cause," the queen replied, "but that is not the greatest wound that pierces my oppressed mind."

No other king or queen of England spilled as much blood in a time of peace as Queen Mary did in four years through her hanging, beheading, burning, and imprisonment of good Christian Englishmen. When she first sought the crown and promised to retain the faith and religion of Edward, God went with her and brought her the throne through the efforts of the Protestants. But after she broke her promises to God and man, sided with Stephen Gardiner, and gave up her supremacy to the pope, God left her. Nothing she did after that thrived.

Instead, she married King Philip and made England subject to a stranger. With Philip came the pope, and his mass, the monks, and the nuns, but still, God prevented her from having her way.

No woman was ever more disappointed than Mary when she could not have children, even with the help of the Catholic Church's prayers. She seemed unable to win the favor of God, the hearts of her subjects, or the love of her husband.

At last, when nothing could sway her to stop the tyranny of her priests and spare her subjects who were being drawn daily as sheep to the slaughter, it pleased God to cut off her rule by death, giving her throne to another after she reigned for five years and five months.

I mentioned this unlucky reign of Queen Mary not to detract from her position, which she was called to by the Lord, but as a warning to men and women in authority who persecute Christ's Church and shed Christian blood, so they will not stumble on the same stone as the Jews who persecuted Christ and His Church, to their own destruction.

The death of Queen Mary seemed to dispel a black, gloomy cloud which for five years had hung like a pall over England. The crowning of Elizabeth was welcomed with joy by the Protestants, and their sufferings during the previous bloody reign were for a moment forgotten in the hope that better days had come.

But Elizabeth, Protestant and friend of the Reformation, loved power as much as her father, Henry VIII, and intended to be no less an absolute ruler of both church and state than he had been. Laws were speedily passed establishing Elizabeth as the supreme head of the church as well as the nation. She was empowered to create a high commission, or court, to try people accused of not taking part in the services of the established Church of England. The power of this court extended over the whole kingdom; the clergy as well as the people were subject to its rule. Any three members of this court could take measures to discover, by summoning witnesses or any other means, anyone who spoke against the queen's supremacy or refused to observe the forms of worship of the established church. They had the power to inquire into any heretical opinions that might be held, to look for seditious books or writings, to try all cases of willful absence from services, and to punish the offenders by fines.

Conclusion

As can be seen, religious liberty, as we know it today, was almost as far as ever from being realized. More than a century would pass before persecution entirely ceased and the passage of a Toleration Act finally established complete freedom of worship in England. But at least Elizabeth was not cruel; aversion to bloodshed was as marked a feature of her character as the reverse had been in that of Mary. The dreadful fires continued for a while longer in Spain and the countries within her grasp, but with the ending of the reign of Queen Mary, the history of English martyrdom was brought to a close.

Inspirational Library

Beautiful purse/pocket-size editions of Christian classics bound in flexible leatherette. These books make thoughtful gifts for everyone on your list, including yourself!

When I'm on My Knees   The highly popular collection of devotional thoughts on prayer, especially for women.
   Flexible Leatherette. $4.97

The Bible Promise Book   Over 1,000 promises from God's Word arranged by topic. What does God promise about matters like: Anger, Illness, Jealousy, Love, Money, Old Age, and Mercy? Find out in this book!
   Flexible Leatherette. $3.97

Daily Wisdom for Women   A daily devotional for women seeking biblical wisdom to apply to their lives. Scripture taken from the New American Standard Version of the Bible.
   Flexible Leatherette. $4.97

My Daily Prayer Journal   Each page is dated and features a Scripture verse and ample room for you to record your thoughts, prayers, and praises. One page for each day of the year.
   Flexible Leatherette. $4.97

Available wherever books are sold.
Or order from:

Barbour Publishing, Inc.
P.O. Box 719
Uhrichsville, OH 44683
http://www.barbourbooks.com

If you order by mail, add $2.00 to your order for shipping.
Prices are subject to change without notice.